The Teen Witches' Guide to

Palm Reading

Written by Xanna Eve Chown

Illustrated by Luna Valentine

ARCTURUS

This edition published in 2022 by Arcturus Publishing Limited
26/27 Bickels Yard, 151–153 Bermondsey Street,
London SE1 3HA

This book was inspired by Johnny Fincham's *Elements: Palmistry*.

Writer: Xanna Eve Chown
Illustrator: Luna Valentine
Designer: Rosie Bellwood
Editor: Donna Gregory

ISBN: 978-1-3988-1519-3
CH010258NT
Supplier 29, Date 0422, Print run 12188

Printed in China

Contents

The Ancient
Art of
Palmistry

Introduction

WHAT ARE YOU LIKE?

Have you ever really taken the time to look at the markings in the palm of your hand? Not even identical twins share the same handprint! Every line is an amazing reminder of how unique you really are. All your qualities, both positive and negative, are marked in your palms and, with a little patience, you can learn how to interpret them. This book will teach you all you need to know. The journey starts here. Let's go!

Palm reading can help you learn more about your personal qualities, such as:
- Do you think about things in a logical way?
- How easy is it for you to show your feelings?
- Are you easy going or anxious?

NO SCARY PREDICTIONS!

In ancient times, when palmistry was used to predict the future, some of the lines and markings on the palm were thought to be bad omens. Luckily, palmistry has evolved since then! Modern palm readers think of it as a tool that can give you valuable insights into your personality. When you look at your hands, it's as if you can look into your mind! So, don't worry if you have an unusual cross or star on your palm. These markings are mostly meaningless, and everyone has the odd squiggle!

No matter what you've heard, a short life line definitely doesn't mean that you will have a short life!

Getting Started

EQUIPMENT

The most important piece of equipment you will need is a magnifying glass, because you can't see the really fine lines without one. Always examine your hand with the glass before you buy it, to make sure you can easily make out your fingerprints. Try to get a magnifying glass with a magnification of around x3, a lens that is the same width as your palm, and, ideally, has a built-in light to highlight the details.

If you have (or can borrow) a good-quality smartphone, you can try taking high-resolution pictures of your palm in good light, and zooming right in to the photo to see the details.

MAKING PRINTS

Making a print of your hand can help you examine the lines in detail. You will need:

- Water-based ink
- A small ink roller
- Plain printer paper
- Newspaper

How to do it:

1. Squeeze a small amount of ink onto a smooth surface and roll the roller over it until it's covered in a thin layer.
2. Roll the roller all over your palm and fingers, coating them in just enough ink to highlight all the lines. If you use too much ink, it will "flood" the lines and make them hard to make out.
3. Place a newspaper under the print paper and press the inked palm down onto the paper with firm pressure.
4. Lift your hand off carefully, holding the printed paper down with one hand while you do so. Don't touch anything else until you've washed your hands!

You will probably need to have a few tries before you get it just right!

The Five Rules of Thumb

Like any practice, palmistry has a set of rules to work by. Take time to memorize these five principles, as they make both study and practical sessions much easier.

1. Don't rush! You must take all the points from both hands into account before you come to any conclusions. Be patient and work carefully through every point.

2. If any finger, line, mount, or marking is common and regular—ignore it. You are only looking for points that show your individuality.

3. Understand that the lines of the palm change through time. People change, grow, and develop, and what is marked in the lines now may not be there next month, next year or in ten years.

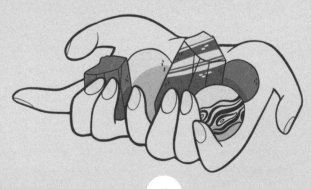

4. There is a positive and negative aspect to every feature on the palm. No exceptions!

5. Palmistry is a caring profession. It is not about impressing people or frightening them. When you are doing a reading, you must be gentle and supportive—even when you are reading for yourself!

ACTIVE AND PASSIVE HANDS

ARE YOU RIGHT- OR LEFT-HANDED?

You always need to examine both hands in a reading, no matter if you are left-handed or right-handed. The hand you throw a ball with is called the active hand, while the one you use less is called the passive hand. Some people are ambidextrous, which means that they are equally good at using both hands. In this case the hand with the stiffest thumb is counted as the active one.

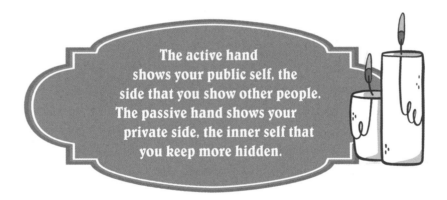

The active hand shows your public self, the side that you show other people. The passive hand shows your private side, the inner self that you keep more hidden.

Imagine two friends. One is your best friend, and the other is someone you only know at school. You know the "active hand" personality of both of them, but you only know the "passive hand" personality of your best friend. (At school, she might be loud and outgoing, but only you know that she is secretly scared of thunderstorms and cries at sad movies!)

14

WHAT'S THE DIFFERENCE?

Always pay attention to the differences between your active and passive hands. These can explain what is happening on the inside that makes you act a certain way on the outside.

(For example, you might meet someone whose active palm shows a strong desire to be famous, but whose passive palm shows a deep sense of insecurity. This might get you thinking—is insecurity at the root of their need for fame?)

In children, the passive palm reflects the personality more strongly. After puberty, the active hand becomes the dominant one.

THE FOUR HAND SHAPES

The first step in palmistry is to look at the overall shape of your palm to see what type it is.

▽ EARTH

Square, heavy palms with short, stiff fingers.

△ AIR

Square palms that are large but lightweight, with long, thin fingers.

▽ WATER

Narrow rectangular palms with long, flexible fingers. They can be pale and cool to the touch.

△ FIRE

Rectangular palms with short fingers. They are often small and warm to the touch. Fire hands are the hardest to identify, as they are a sort of "middling" hand.

> **Some people have palms that don't fall into any category. If this is case, simply ignore the hand shape and move on to the next step!**

▽ EARTH

△ AIR

▽ WATER

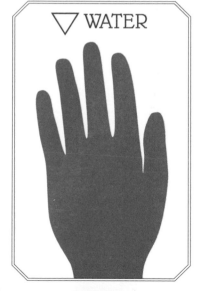

△ FIRE

WHAT'S YOUR HAND TYPE?

Earth hands

You are strong and practical and would rather be doing something active than just sitting around. You love your home and family, and you adore animals. Sometimes you worry that people take you for granted, but—just like the earth beneath your feet—you know that you are essential!

EARTH PROFESSIONS:
- **Hairdresser**
- **Chef**
- **Farmer**
- **Engineer**

Air hands

You love to think, talk, and teach—but you also have a tendency to daydream. You enjoy learning and may have one special area of interest that you know everything about. You hate unfairness of any description. You might find you move your hands a lot while talking,

AIR PROFESSIONS:
- **Comedian**
- **Writer**
- **Teacher**
- **Entertainer**

Fire hands

You are full of energy and can get frustrated when you think other people are being lazy! You are happy taking risks to achieve your goals and are quick to adapt to new trends and skills. You are drawn to situations where excitement and drama are found. You wear clothes that help you stand out from the crowd!

FIRE PROFESSIONS:
- **Media personality**
- **Actor**
- **Sports player**
- **Entrepreneur**

Water hands

Those who don't know you may think you are secretive or moody, but you are naturally caring and compassionate. You are fascinated by magic and mystery and love to explore relationships and feelings. You are a great artist and enjoy expressing yourself in creative ways. You may find that you change your mind a lot!

WATER PROFESSIONS:
- **Nursery teacher**
- **Vet**
- **Nurse**
- **Artist**

Skin Texture

The skin on the inner palm is very important in palmistry. The hands contain some of the densest areas of nerve endings in the body, which means that they are very sensitive to touch. To find out your skin type, stroke the centre of your left palm with the index finger of your right hand. (This is your most sensitive fingertip!)

As a palmist, you need to be able to feel the differences in skin texture. You can do this by running your finger over the inner palms of your some of your friends and family members. (Ask their permission first!) Notice the differences between them and think about how their skin type reflects their personality. For example, are they shy or outgoing? Arty or sporty? Chatty or quiet?

WHAT'S YOUR SKIN TYPE?

Palmists divide the skin on the inner palm into four categories. The most rough and hard is "coarse", next comes "grainy," then "paper," and lastly, "silk," the most fine and sensitive. Someone who does a lot of work with their hands, such as building or gardening, may have hard callouses, or rough patches, on their palms, but this won't affect their skin type.

People in their eighties and beyond tend to have very fine skin on the inner palm. This is because skin becomes thin in old age, making it harder to judge its texture.

Silk

- You have very fine skin.
- The skin ridges are so densely packed that you can't feel them at all.
- You have many fine scratchy lines all over the palm.

You are very sensitive, and highly aware of touch, temperature and other people's moods. You try to avoid competition and harsh environments. You may be prone to allergies.

Paper

- You have fine, dry skin, often slightly yellowish.
- The skin ridges can just be perceived.
- There are quite a number of lines on the palm.
- This is the most common skin type.

You like connecting to others through books, computers and phones. You can be a little distant and sometimes are wary of physical touch.

Grainy

- Your skin ridges are clearly visible and easily felt.
- The lines on the palm are deep, red, and easily seen, like cuts.
- Your palm has a slightly hard feel to it.

You always like to be busy and are restless when you are inactive. You love sports, martial arts, or dancing. You don't spend a lot of time looking inward or reflecting on things.

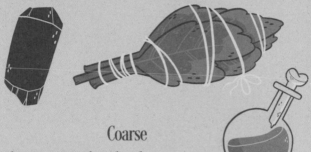

Coarse

- Coarse skin is immediately obvious.
- Your palm feels very hard and very rough
- There are very few lines, and the lines are deep grooves.

You love to be outdoors and need to be physically active. You are incredibly hardy and resilient but may not be very sensitive to other people's feelings.

Fingers

WHAT'S UNIQUE ABOUT YOUR FINGERS?

When you examine the fingers, you're bound to discover something really interesting—whether that's length, stiffness, or print pattern. The fingers identify your character traits and can even reflect your upbringing! They reveal what's going on in the more modern, developed parts of your brain.

The fingers aren't completely formed until the late teens, so keep studying your fingers regularly, noting any changes you see.

CHECK YOUR FINGERS!

Finger flexibility equals mental flexibility! Stiffness of the fingers is checked by simply placing the palm of one hand against the fingertips of the other and gently pushing all the fingers back toward the wrist.

Stiff?

Fingers which hardly move back when you push against them suggest very rigid mental processes. You probably prefer routine to spontaneity.

Flexible?

If the fingers pull back by up to 7 cm (3 in.), this is normal and not worth noting.

Very flexible?

If the fingers are floppy and bend back 45 degrees or more, you have a spontaneous and impulsive mind. You are open to new ideas but may find it hard to stick to any opinion for long!

NAMING THE FINGERS

Ancient palmists used the planets to describe the qualities of each finger, but modern palm readers use metaphors for the fingers to make their qualities easy to understand.

- **Mirror finger.** Just as you see your reflection in a mirror, this finger reflects your identity.
- **Wall finger.** This finger is all about your values, career, family, and friends. Think of these as the bricks that make up a sturdy wall!
- **Peacock finger.** Just as a peacock expresses itself with its flamboyant tail, this finger shows how you express yourself.
- **Antenna finger.** This finger describes how you communicate. Think of the way an antenna on a radio transmits and receives signals.
- **Thumb.** Strictly speaking, your thumb is a digit, not a finger! It shows your will power and reason.

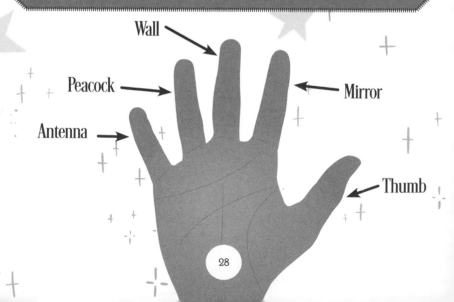

Wall

Peacock

Antenna

Mirror

Thumb

ARE YOUR FINGERS LONG OR SHORT?

It's very common to have at least one finger extra-long, extra short or bent. Whenever a finger is long or short, it will be like this on both hands. Remember, you're looking at how long your fingers are compared to each other—not compared to your friends!

Rest a ruler horizontally at the tip of your mirror finger, pushing your wall finger slightly behind it.

- If the mirror finger is slightly shorter than the peacock, this is considered average. If it is the same length as the peacock or longer, it's considered long. If it is more than 2 mm (1/16 in.) shorter than the peacock, it's considered short.
- If the wall finger has almost half its top section (from the tip of the finger to the first crease) above the ruler, it's considered average.
- The antenna finger usually comes up to the top crease of the peacock finger.

THE THUMB

The thumb is expressive of your self-control and drive.
You can tell a lot by its flexibility and length! To check
the flexibility of your thumb, push it back toward your
wrist. It will always be a little stiffer on your active hand.
Most thumbs move back by 1 cm (½ in.) or so. If your
thumb bends back almost to the wrist, it's flexible. If it
won't bend back at all, it's stiff.

Very flexible

You are easy-going and laid-back. You tend to
only work hard when you are doing something
you enjoy—and hate pushing yourself too hard.

Very stiff

You are very stiff in your resolve. This means
that when you have decided on a course of
action, you stick to it. You are very persistent
and like to stick to your goals. You don't
bend easily to other people's will.

HOW LONG IS YOUR THUMB?

The length of the thumb is measured by laying it against the base of the mirror finger. If the tip comes up to anywhere along the bottom section of the mirror finger, then it's considered average.

Tall

If your thumb makes it to the first joint line of your mirror finger it shows that you have huge reserves of will power, great drive, and energy. You don't enjoy being around lazy people!

Short

If your thumb doesn't make it to the base of the mirror finger, it shows that you have trouble motivating yourself. You should take care not to let yourself be controlled by other, more forceful people.

If you look at the thumbs of people with great self-discipline, like Olympic athletes and professional footballers, you'll often see a long, stiff thumb.

Mirror Finger

The mirror finger is the most important finger in palmistry. Even the slightest bend, length variation or unusual print pattern in this finger will make a massive difference to your personality. If it bends toward the wall finger, it shows that you have a strong need to belong, both at home and at school.

The mirror finger tells you about your:

Self-esteem — How much confidence do you have in yourself?

Integrity — How honest and fair you are?

Responsibility — Can you take care of yourself and others?

Ambition — Do you have dreams and goals that you want to achieve?

Sense of power — Can you stand up for yourself and what you believe in?

HOW LONG IS YOUR MIRROR FINGER?

Long

- You like to take control of situations and can sometimes be a bit bossy!
- You are very capable and always exceed expectations.
- You don't like to fail or get things wrong.
- You are very ambitious and have a lot of goals for the future.

Short

- You do not have much confidence in your abilities.
- You don't like taking on too much responsibility.
- You don't spend much time thinking about why you do things.
- You sometimes find it hard to stand up for yourself.

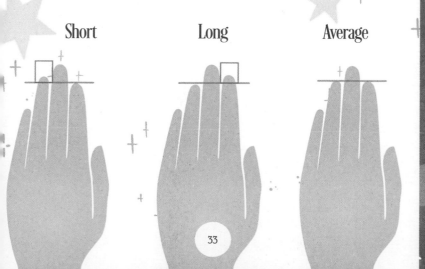

Short   **Long**   **Average**

WALL FINGER

This is the longest finger. It shows the parts of your personality that help you find your place in the world around you. When the wall finger bends, it's usually in the direction of the peacock finger. This can show that you are finding your family or school life too demanding, and long to live a more fun-filled, carefree life!

The wall finger tells you about your:

Sense of belonging — How well do you fit in with different groups, such as family or friends?

Vocation — What sort of job or career are you drawn to?

Religion — What do you believe in?

Codes of behaviour — How well do you fit in with other people's expectations?

Boundaries — What do you find acceptable and unacceptable?

HOW LONG IS YOUR WALL FINGER?

Short

- You may struggle to accept your family's values.
- You think that your family is too strict with their rules—or not strict enough!
- You may wish for a more alternative lifestyle.
- You find it hard to belong.
- You like to challenge the rules.

Long

- There are some things in life that you take seriously, such as work, family or religion.
- You always like to know about the details.
- You are interested in getting good grades at school.
- You believe you have a duty to society.
- You are drawn to scientific or academic worlds.

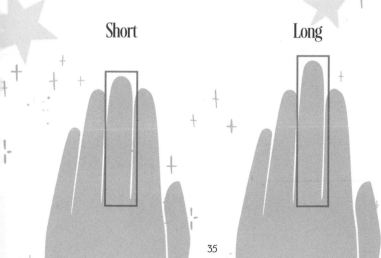

Short   Long

Peacock Finger

This finger is about your public image, the side of you that other people can see. When the peacock finger bends, it will be in the direction of the wall finger. This can show that you care a lot about how you appear to other people.

> **The peacock finger tells you about your:**
>
> **Popularity**   How important is it for you to be appreciated by others?
>
> **Competitiveness**   How strong is your drive to compete, excel and stand out?

HOW LONG IS YOUR PEACOCK FINGER?

Long

- You have a strong desire to be make an impression and be noticed by other people.
- You may like to go to extremes when it comes to the clothes you wear and your hairstyle.
- You like to perform, whether you are acting, dancing or playing sport.
- You enjoy taking risks and challenging yourself.

Short

- You would rather be respected than popular.
- You love to be creative, but you do not enjoy showing off to others.
- You are very aware of how other people might see you.

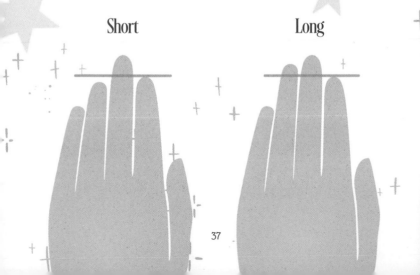

Short   Long

Antenna Finger

The antenna finger is all communication at every level. If the antenna finger bends, it's always inward, toward the peacock finger. This means that you are good at using words to convince other people of something (whether it is true or not!)

The antenna finger tells you about your:

Wit	Are you a quick thinker? What sort of things do you find funny?
Charm	Do you find it easy to make other people like you?
Language abilities	Do you find it easy to talk to people on a range of subjects?

- Children always have a low-set antenna finger, where the first crease line on the antenna is at the same level as the base of the peacock finger, or lower.
- During puberty, this finger is usually pushed upward so the first crease line is halfway up the bottom phalange of the peacock finger. However, on around a quarter of adults, this finger stays low set.

- A long antenna finger can initially appear short if it's low set in the palm. In such cases, add an imaginary 1 cm (½ in.) to the tip of the finger!

HOW LONG IS YOUR ANTENNA FINGER?

Long

- You have a natural skill with language and probably learned to read at an early age.
- You may be drawn to jobs that involve writing, teaching, sales, and marketing.
- You enjoy telling jokes, especially puns!

Short

- You prefer to use simple, direct language.
- You don't always understand when other people are being sarcastic.
- You prefer practical jokes to puns.

Print
Patterns

Print Patterns on the Fingers

The fingerprints are very important in modern palmistry. They can't tell you what you're thinking, but they can help you understand how you think. To see them better, it might help to make prints on paper with ink.

The scientific word for the print patterns is "dermatoglyphics" which comes from the Greek "derma" for skin and "glyph" for markings.

The most common prints on the fingers are called ulnar loops. If you have these, it is not worth mentioning in a reading. But whenever you find something different, it's a powerful character trait! It's important to remember that the meanings of the print patterns only affect the area that they are found on. For example—a whorl on a mirror finger will mean something different from a whorl on a thumb!

The five types of print pattern:
- **Whorl**
- **Simple arch**
- **Tented arch**
- **Loop**
- **Composite (double loop)**

WHAT DO THE PRINT PATTERNS MEAN?

Whorl prints

The whorl print is made of a series of ever-decreasing circles or a spiral which curls into itself. Sometimes there are a few loop lines wrapped around the whorl. The whorl is seen a lot on creative people, such as artists. Whorls on many fingers suggest that you follow your own ideas, rather than following trends.

Whorls show that:
- You have a need for space and privacy.
- You enjoy working alone.
- You prefer to focus on one subject rather than have a lot of different skills.

Simple arch prints

The simple arch is made of a series of upside-down V-shaped lines piled on top of each other. This pattern shows you are very good at working with your hands.

Simple arches show that:
- You are practical, dependable, and loyal.
- It can be hard for you to show sadness or anger in front of others.
- You have a powerful drive to protect people, animals, and nature.

Tented arches

Tented arches form a distinctive spike formation that looks like a tent pole with the lines pushed up around it. This pattern is seen on people who like exciting or even dangerous jobs. (Think stunt performer, athlete, alligator wrangler ...)

Tented arches show that:

- You have an intense personality.
- You love to dramatize, shock, and excite—you are never boring!
- You like to push yourself to extremes and are very adventurous.

Loop prints

Ulnar loops are thrown in the direction of the thumb, and they rise and fall like a wave. This is the most common pattern on the fingers.

Ulnar loops show that:
- You are happiest when you feel like you fit in.
- You prioritize friendships and relationships.
- You have a strong empathy for your environment.

Radial loop

When you find a loop moving in the opposite direction to the common ulnar loop, it's known as a radial loop. (It's easy to see the difference as the radial loop moves away from the thumb!) People with these loops tend to enjoy careers that involve looking after others.

Radial loops show that:

- You are very aware of other people's needs.
- You hate being criticized and need to be liked by other people.
- You have a great ability to connect with others.

Composite

The composite is formed by two loops going in opposite directions, like a yin-yang symbol. This sign appears on people with have to examine all the sides of an issue. For example, a lawyer, a therapist, or a teacher.

Composites show that:
- You sometimes doubt your own decisions.
- You are interested in spirituality and philosophy.
- You can be neutral.

WHICH PATTERNS CAN YOU SEE ON YOUR MIRROR FINGER?

The mirror finger is the one most likely to show a non-ulnar loop. It is the most important finger and should always be the first one you examine.

Whorl:

- You are an individual, with unusual interests and hobbies.
- You are intelligent and thoughtful.
- You are happy spending time alone and hate crowds.

Simple arch:

- People see you as reliable.
- You can be a little stubborn.
- You love nature and animals, and your family.

Radial loop:

- You can be a little insecure and you hate criticism.
- You are very aware of other people's feelings.
- You are great at connecting with others.

Composite:

- You are a deep thinker.
- You can find it tricky to make decisions.
- You are a very good diplomat.

Tented arch:

- You are intense and dramatic.
- You like to entertain or teach.
- You have loads of charisma and charm.

WHICH PATTERNS CAN YOU SEE ON YOUR THUMB?

Whorl:

- You are independent and you like people to know it!
- You have lots of original ideas.
- You like to feel that you are always making yourself a better person.

Simple arch:

- You can be very stubborn.
- You are practical and not afraid to get your hands dirty.
- You don't like taking risks.

Composite:

- You often change your mind.
- You can be hesitant about committing to anything.
- You are good at multitasking!

WHICH PATTERNS CAN YOU SEE ON YOUR WALL FINGER?

Whorl:

- You aren't a big fan of tradition, and you often question the rules.
- You have unusual interests and hobbies.
- You sometimes disagree with your parents about their beliefs.

Simple arch:

- You have a serious attitude toward your work.
- You have a strong sense of fairness.
- You like order—and you don't like mess!

Radial loop:

- You are always changing your ideas about things that you like and don't like.
- You find it easy to fit in with other people.
- You may be drawn to very alternative lifestyles.

Composite:

- You are always challenging your own beliefs.
- You can't settle on the sort of job that you would like. (Too many interesting options!)
- You like to learn about different cultures.

WHICH PATTERNS CAN YOU SEE ON YOUR PEACOCK FINGER?

Whorl:

- You are a visual person, who is very interested in the way things look.
- You have a flair for design.
- You may have an unusual taste in clothes and music.

Simple arch:

- You love to express yourself through hugs!
- You love learning about history.
- You like to wear simple, stylish clothes.

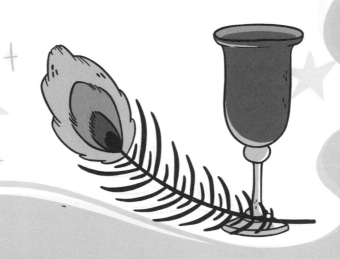

WHICH PATTERNS CAN YOU SEE ON YOUR ANTENNA FINGER?

Whorl:

- You like to learn new words and even technical jargon.
- You are very secretive about who you have a crush on!
- You may have some unusual friends.

Simple arch:

- You find it easy to talk to both adults and younger children.
- You don't like it when people invade your personal space.
- You enjoy sharing your knowledge by teaching.

Patterns on the Palms

Interpreting the Prints
on the Palm

THE QUADRANTS

Imagine your palm is split into four, unequal zones. Each zone relates to a different aspect of your brain. Whenever you see a line, print, or marking, it can only relate to the zone it's found on.

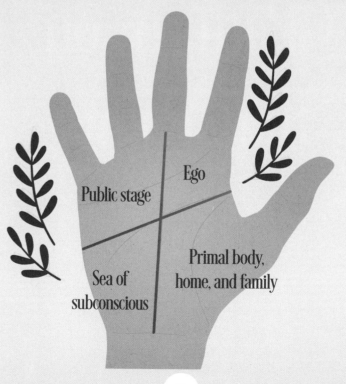

Public stage

Ego

Sea of subconscious

Primal body, home, and family

Sea of subconscious

The area at the base of your hand is all about your dreams, intuition, deep fears and desires, and spiritual connection.

Public stage

The area on the side of your antenna finger tells you about your need to connect to the wider world.

Ego

Your ego is your sense of self. The area on the side of your mirror finger describes ambition and self-development.

Primal body, home, and family

Primal means earliest, or original. This area tells you about your foundations, where you come from, and where you find security.

If you want to make a guess at the meaning of a marking, take a look at where it appears on your hand.

- Crosses suggest two opposing energies and the need to make a decision.
- Stars show many possible options and can mean that a new opportunity is on the horizon.
- Forks and tridents at the end of a line show the ability to function on more than one level.

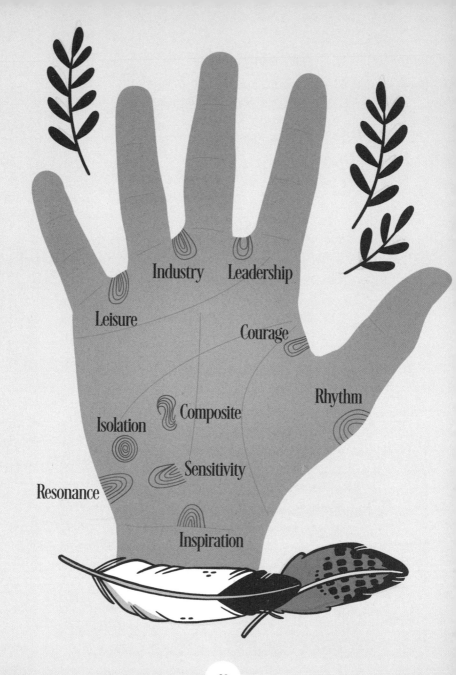

Industry   Leadership

Leisure

Courage

Rhythm

Isolation   Composite

Sensitivity

Resonance

Inspiration

INTERFINGERAL LOOPS

These are little loops that form at the point where the
fingers are joined by a web of skin.

Loop of leisure
This is a common marking that shows you prefer leisure
activities to work—and adore time off school or a job!

Loop of industry
This is a common marking that shows you take your work
seriously and have a strong sense of duty.

Loop of leadership
This is a rare marking that means you are great at
organization and are a natural manager.

OTHER MARKINGS ON THE PALM

Loop of sensitivity

You have a strong psychic ability and can pick up on feelings that are hidden to others.

Whorl of isolation

You are unreachable in terms of your inner, deeper personality. You need to be private and alone a great deal. This is a strongly creative marking, often found on writers and actors.

Loop of resonance

You have a powerful love of the natural world and may have a gift for healing. You can feel the Earth's energy and are fascinated with mystery, magic and the unknown.

Composite on sea of subconscious

This is a very rare marking. You often feel like you are on an emotional rollercoaster! You love to learn about psychology and the way that people think.

Loop of inspiration

You are an artist, musician or spiritual seekers who is fascinated by dreams and open to mystical experiences.

Loop of rhythm

You have a strong sense of rhythm and a love of music. The need to dance and listen to music is deep in your bones!

Loop of courage

You are driven and competitive and seek out challenges. This marking is very common on sportspeople and martial artists.

Major Lines

Heart, Head, Fate, Life

There are four major lines, and they are by far the most important ones on the palm. They slowly change and develop throughout your lifetime. If a major line is of average length and form, it's not important. But if a major line is unusual in its length or form, weak, broken, or missing, then it is worth taking a closer look. All major lines start at the same point in the palm, but they vary hugely in where they end.

You should always read the lines of the palm after observing skin texture and print patterns. This will mean you have already established any major character traits and the lines are read in the context of these qualities. Always note differences between the active and passive hands.

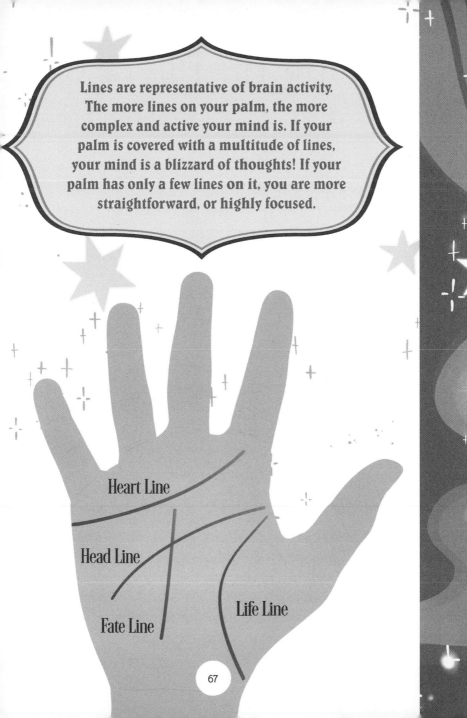

Lines are representative of brain activity. The more lines on your palm, the more complex and active your mind is. If your palm is covered with a multitude of lines, your mind is a blizzard of thoughts! If your palm has only a few lines on it, you are more straightforward, or highly focused.

Heart Line

Head Line

Fate Line

Life Line

THE LIFE LINE

The life line should be clear and strong, beginning above the thumb and running in a semicircle around the thumb ball to the base of the palm. If it has a wide sweep, you have enormous energy and lust for life. If the line is almost straight and stays very close to the thumb, you are likely to be more cautious.

The life line shows your:

Stability	Does your life feel crazy or calm?
Sense of security	How much trust do you have in yourself and the world?
Practicality	Are you a thinker or a do-er?
Physical vitality	Are you full of energy or always tired?

In medieval times the life line was thought to show the length of a person's life. However, this has long been disproved. There are many people in their nineties with short life lines!

WHAT DOES YOUR LIFE LINE LOOK LIKE?

Short

- You are a bit of a dreamer, who tends to flit between projects and interests.
- You have a strong drive to achieve wealth, power and influence.

Weak

- You can be a little insecure.
- You desire a life of power and influence.

Forked

- This is called a travel line.
- It shows that you have an adventurous spirit and would love to wander the world.

Broken

- You have been through some big life changes, such as parental separation, moving house, or bad health.
- Often the line is stronger after the break, which shows your positive energy returning after the crisis has passed.

THE HEAD LINE

The head line starts near the top of the life line and is sometimes connected to it. A long head line ends close to the opposite edge of the palm, but a short line ends beneath the wall finger. An average line usually ends under the peacock finger.

The head line shows your mental focus. A fuzzy head line can suggest that you are finding life quite stressful. If this is the case, it can be strengthened by spending time focusing on simple, practical tasks, such as cooking or gardening.

WHAT DOES YOUR HEAD LINE LOOK LIKE?

Long

- You're a deep thinker, and probably have a love of learning.
- You spend a lot of time thinking about the future.

Short

- You tend to focus on the here and now, which makes you very productive.
- You are always learning new skills and don't waste too much time worrying.

Straight

- You are level-headed and rational and tend to think in a logical way.
- You like facts and tend to only believe in something if you have experienced it.

Bent

- The head line always bends downward.
- You are likely to love mystical things, and have a vivid artistic imagination.

71

Clear

- If the line is clear and without breaks, it shows that you have amazing powers of concentration!

Broken

- Islands, breaks, or fuzzy areas mean you can sometimes be a bit disorganized or find it hard to focus.

Crosses the palm

- When the line completely crosses the palm, effectively cutting it in half, this is known as a Sydney line.
- This is associated with high intelligence and brain power, as well as difficulty sleeping!
- It is common in people with ADHD and dyslexia.

Forked

- A branch at the end of the head line is known as a "writer's fork."
- It shows a versatile and inspirational mind, which is good at problem-solving.

Close to the life line

- If the head line stays stuck to the lifelife, you may not have much confidence in your own opinions.
- This is often seen on people who have strict parents or go to a strict school!

Far from the life line

- A large space between the beginning of the head line and the life line shows that you are adventurous and independent.

THE HEART LINE

This line begins under the antenna finger and usually ends somewhere between the mirror or peacock finger.

> **The heart line tells you about your emotional responses. The deeper, darker, and longer the line is, the more emotional energy you have.**

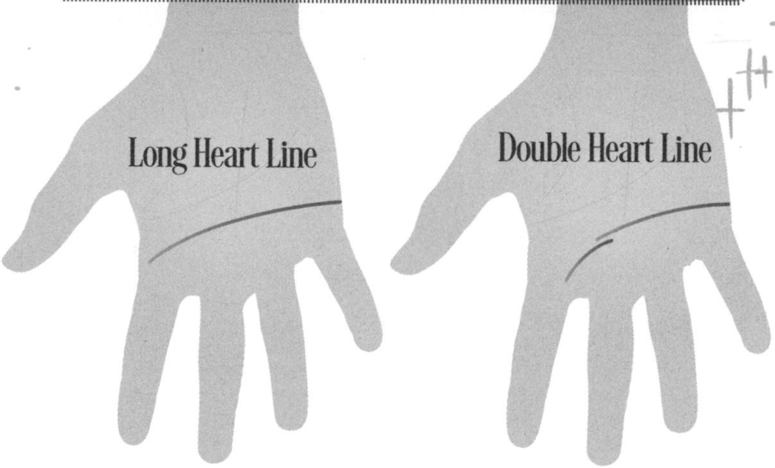

Long Heart Line

Double Heart Line

WHAT DOES YOUR HEART LINE LOOK LIKE?

Long

- A long heart line ends very close to the edge of the palm below the mirror finger.
- You have a long list of friends and would do anything for them.

- If the line crosses the palm completely from side to side, it shows that you can be intense in your relationships —which can sometimes lead to you getting hurt.

Short

- A short line ends somewhere under the wall finger.
- You have a small circle of friends and may prefer animals to people!

Broken

- A messy heart line means that you tend toward emotional extremes.
- You either pour all your feelings out—or keep them all bottled in!

Curving upward

- You are very romantic and enjoy expressing your feelings.

Straight

- You express your emotions in a practical way. For example, running errands or buying gifts.
- This is a good sign on a parent or partner, as it shows you are very nurturing.

Split

- Sometimes the heart line splits in two with a higher and lower section, meaning that you have two sides to your personality.

THE FATE LINE

The fate line runs vertically up the middle of the palm and always runs toward the wall finger. This line can be difficult to identify because it can take several forms. It can start from the middle of the palm, or from the life line, or from the sea of subconscious.

The fate line shows how much energy you put into your personal goals and beliefs. Always compare the active and passive hands as they are often very different.

Fate Line

It's normal for this line to be only partially present until you are in your twenties or early thirties.

HOW DOES YOUR FATE LINE LOOK?

Straight

- You are mature and well balanced.
- You have a straightforward approach to life and know how to stand up for yourself.

Faint

- You need time to work out what you want.
- At times, you may feel very anxious.

Starts in the sea of subconscious

- You love working with other people and using your creativity.
- You tend toward a non-traditional lifestyle.

Joined to the life line

- You enjoy security and have a need for a happy family.
- You may choose to spend a long time in education.

Starts halfway up the palm

- You may change your direction midway through life
- You will find positive changes as you discover more about who you are and what you want.

Runs all the way up the palm

- It is rare for this line to run from the very bottom to the base of the wall finger, but when it does, it shows that you are inflexible and like everything to stay the same.

BREAKS, ISLANDS, BAR LINES, AND DUPLICATES

All the major lines may break and re-form. They may have an island somewhere along their length, or have a short bar line crossing them. Sometimes the line is doubled, although this is rare.

Any markings on the lines relate to the area of life that is shown by the line:

Life line—your home, health, or family.
Heart line—your emotional life.
Fate line—your work and the direction of your life.
Head line—your personality and way of thinking.

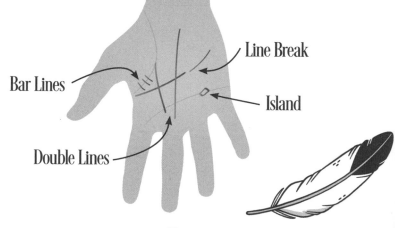

Bar Lines

Line Break

Island

Double Lines

DO THE LINES ON YOUR HAND HAVE ANY OF THESE?

Breaks

- A break anywhere on a major line shows a big life change.
- If the line becomes stronger after the break, there has been a positive outcome.
- If the line becomes weaker after the break, it shows that you still need support.

Islands

- When an island is seen, you always need to de-stress.
- You may be feeling confused about a situation.

Bar lines

- These occur where a short line crosses a major line and show that you have obstacles to be overcome.
- Where there are a series of bar lines, it's a sign for you to change your approach to these obstacles.

Doubled lines

- You are a complex, changeable person.
- You find it easy to switch between two different ways of being—for example you act differently at home and at school.

Minor Lines

Meet the Minor Lines

- The minor lines are far fainter and scratchier than the major lines.
- They vary a lot in their formation and can change very quickly—sometimes in a matter of days or weeks.
- Remember that it's perfectly normal not to see any particular minor line. Some people have none at all!
- Always consider which hand the minor line shows up on the most. If it is strongest on your active hand, it affects your outer life, but if it is strongest on your passive hand, it affects your inner life.

Very rarely, you'll see a minor line that's really deep and red and stronger than any of the major lines. This shows that your life is not balanced. You are pouring all your energy into one thing. This could mean that you are naturally gifted in one area—or it could mean that you need to make a few changes to get things back in balance!

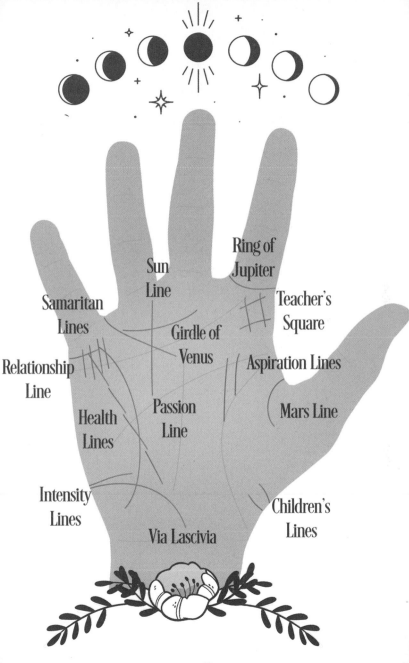

Sun
Line

Ring of
Jupiter

Teacher's
Square

Samaritan
Lines

Girdle of
Venus

Relationship
Line

Aspiration Lines

Health
Lines

Passion
Line

Mars Line

Intensity
Lines

Children's
Lines

Via Lascivia

Sun Line

This line is very fine and runs vertically up to the base of the peacock finger. It's nearly always seen above the heart line. If this is the case, it is unremarkable. However, if the line runs below the heart line for 2.5 cm (1 in.) or more, it's very significant.

- If your sun line runs below your heart line, it shows that you have the rare ability to be deeply content without attention from others.
- The traditional Indian study of palmistry teaches that a strong Sun line indicates wealth and good fortune!

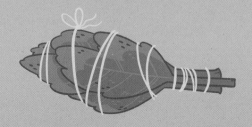

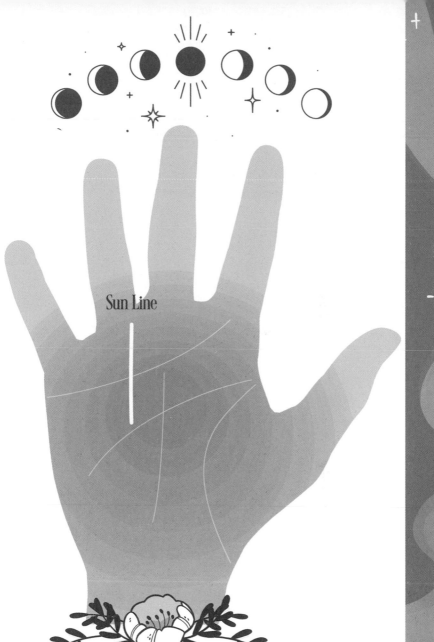

Sun Line

CHILDREN'S LINES

These show up as short, bold lines in the home, family, and body quadrant on the active hand.

- **They appear when children are present in the home—they are not a prediction of future offspring!**
- **Curved lines often represent girls and straight lines often indicate boys.**

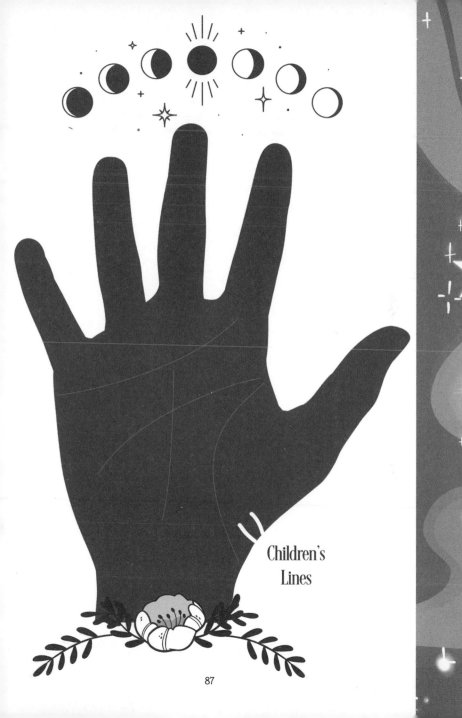

Children's
Lines

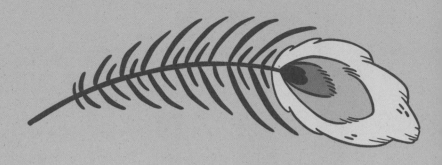

GIRDLE OF VENUS

This is a line or series of parallel lines floating above the heart line.

- You are a bit of a daydreamer and love books and movies that transport you to other worlds.
- You often feel the need to escape and might live somewhere else that's a bit more luxurious!
- You have a sense of wonder and a love of the arts—whether that's drama, music, or books.

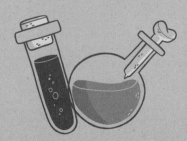

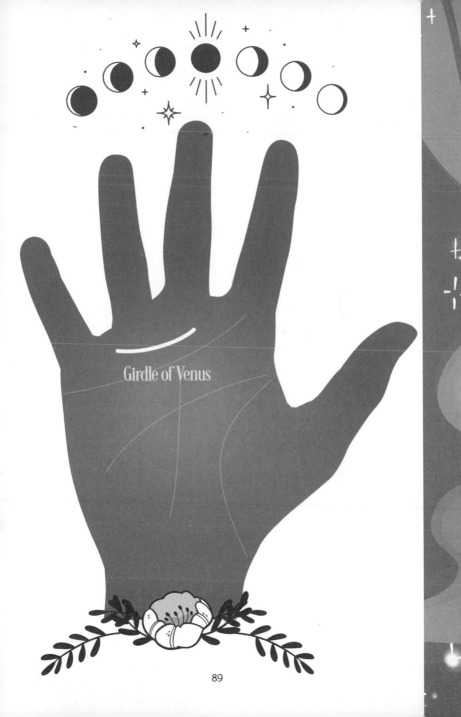

Girdle of Venus

HEALTH LINE

Health lines are difficult to identify as they are almost always
a series of random, vertical scratchy lines running anywhere
from the base of the life line to the base of the antenna finger.
Sometimes there are four or five fine lines running together,
sometimes a sort of ladder effect and, occasionally,
just one thin line.

- **The stronger the line, the more likely you are to be stressed.**
- **If your health line shows that you are stressed, take time to think about what you can do to calm your body down.**
- **Activities that involve slow, deep breathing such as meditation and yoga can work wonders on the health line!**

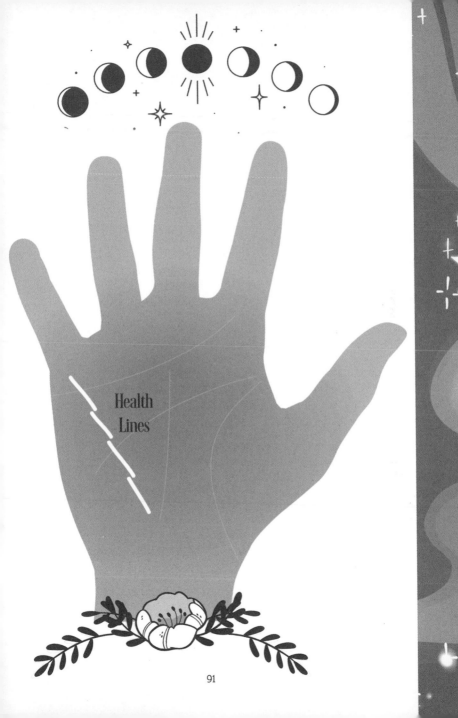

Health
Lines

Intuition Line

The intuition line is curved, complete, and very fine. It's quite easy to get this line confused with the health line as it is found in the same area of the palm.

This line is common on people with strong psychic abilities. You might be the sort of person who often has "hunches" about people or situations that are proved right!

Intuition
Line

Relationship Line

Relationship lines are found on the outer edge of the palm below the antenna finger and above the heart line. These lines can be ignored unless they are long—for example, running for 2.5 cm (1 in.) or more under the antenna finger.

- If a relationship line is long and curves upward to cut around the base of the antenna finger, it's likely that you do not find it easy to trust other people.
- If the line is long and straight, you may find that you hold back from relationships until you are older and have more experience of the world.

There is a myth that these lines show the number of marriages and children you will have. This is nonsense, as almost everyone has one or two of these markings.

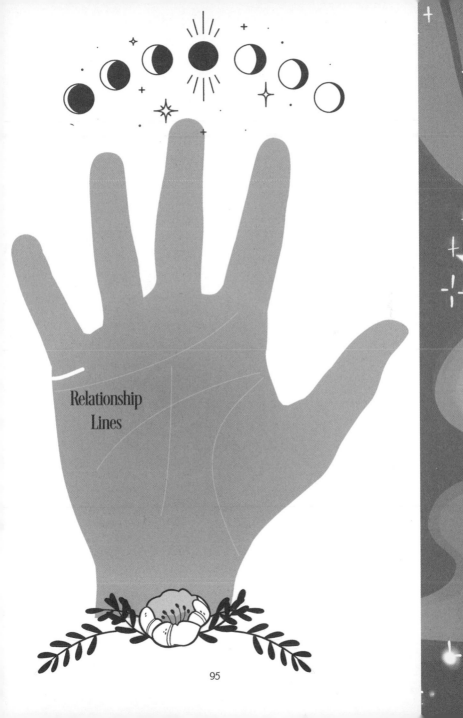

Relationship
Lines

Ring of Jupiter

This forms a semi-circle around the base of the mirror finger. Be careful not to confuse it with the normal crease or double crease that is always present at the bottom of this finger. The true line is very fine, semicircular, and runs below the crease.

- It shows that you have a strong interest in other people and find it easy to understand their thoughts and feelings.
- Your friends know that you are a good listener, and often come to you with their problems. If the line is strong, it shows that you are very intelligent.
- It is said that if there are two rings here you are exceptionally lucky!
- This sign is very rarely seen—but it is surprisingly common on palm readers!

This line is sometimes called the Ring of Solomon. In the Bible, King Solomon was famous for his wisdom!

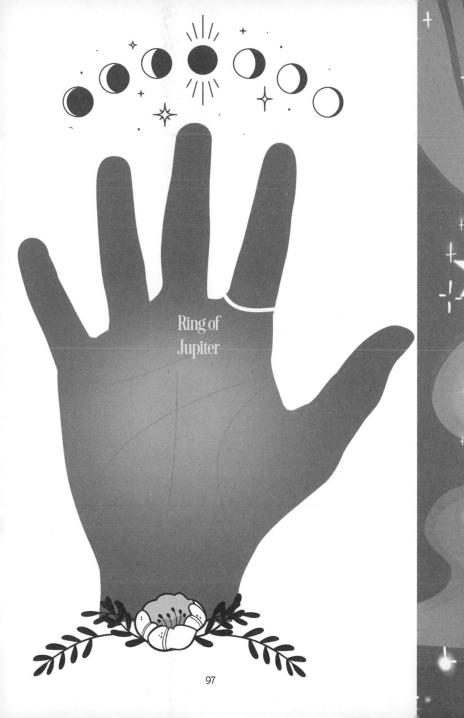

Ring of
Jupiter

TEACHER'S SQUARE

These aren't really true squares, but a formation of four intersecting markings under the mirror finger.

- **You are good at managing other people and are a very patient teacher.**
- **You shine when it comes to passing on your skills and knowledge to others.**

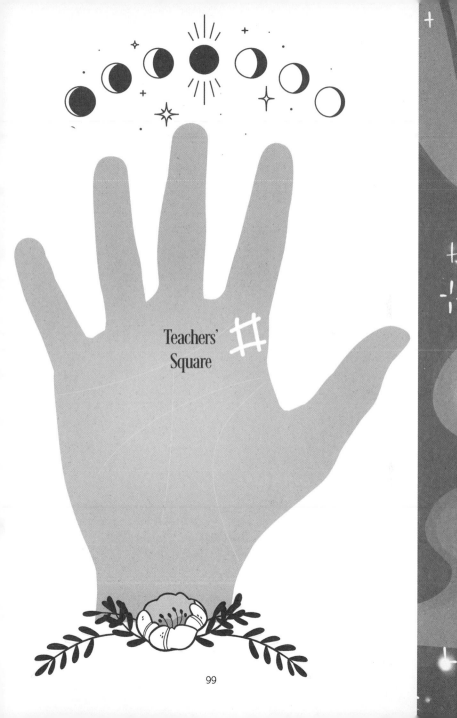

Teachers'
Square

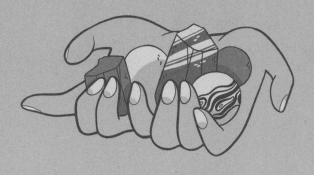

Samaritan Lines

These are a series of thin lines running vertically in
the area around the base of the antenna finger.

- These lines show that you love to do good, and spend
  time caring for others.
- If there are four or more lines, it suggests that you are a
  good neighbour and have a strong community spirit.
- These markings were once thought to show that someone
  had magical or healing hands.

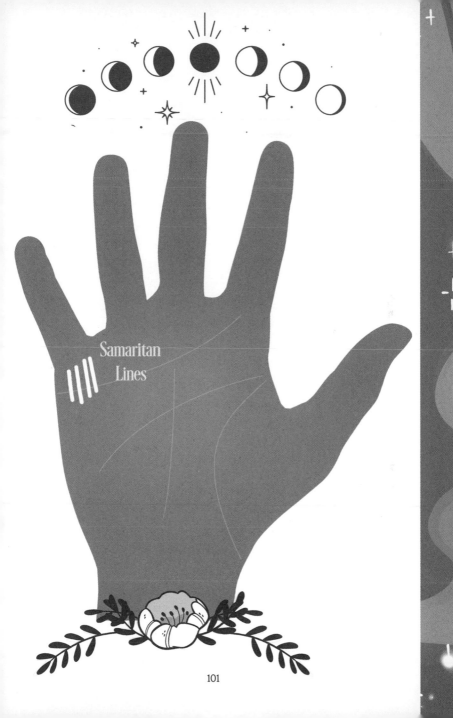

Samaritan
Lines

Companion Lines

These fragile lines are found inside the life line.

- Most people have a number of these, and they represent the people close to you.
- The passive hand shows your siblings and the active hand shows your best friends.
- When there are many lines, it means that you have a large and complex group of relationships.
- Sometimes when these lines seem to stop suddenly, with a cross or island at the end, they show that a relationship has ended.

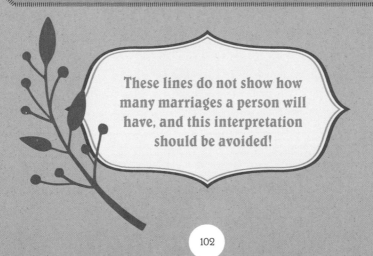

These lines do not show how many marriages a person will have, and this interpretation should be avoided!

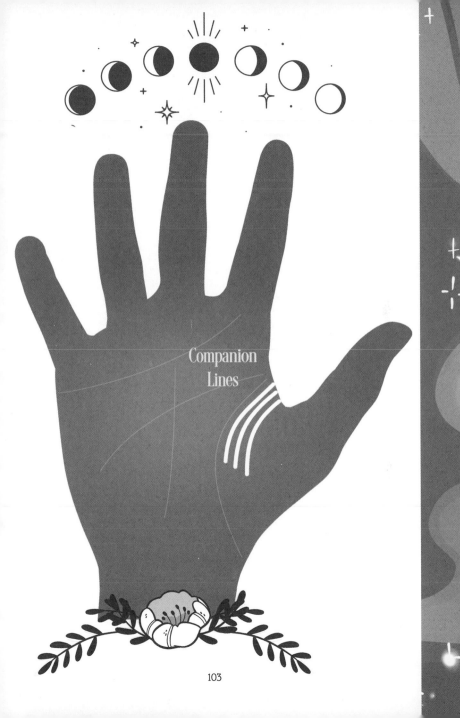

Companion
Lines

Aspiration Lines

These are fine, hairlike lines rising up from your life line pointing toward your mirror finger.

- Your aspirations are your hopes and ambitions.
- If you have these lines, it can show that you are always trying to learn new things and improve yourself.
- You have a lot of drive and energy to succeed. If you are on a mission to be the best "you" possible then you are likely to succeed!

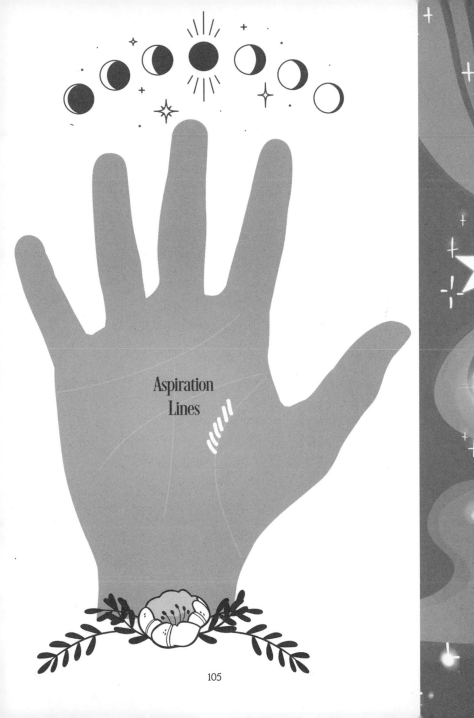

Aspiration
Lines

Mars Line

The Mars line is rare, and found within the upper part of the life line, close to the thumb. Only if clear and strong and longer than 1 cm (½ in.) is it worthy of note—most people have a short, scratchy line here.

- You have tons of energy, a competitive nature, and the need for challenges.
- You probably love sports, gymnastics, dancing, or martial arts.
- You will often find this line on the hands of top sports stars!

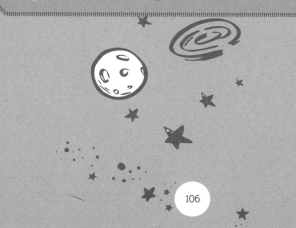

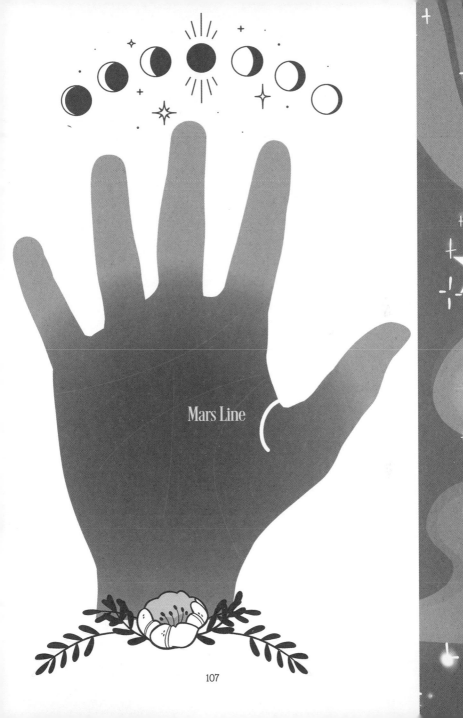

Mars Line

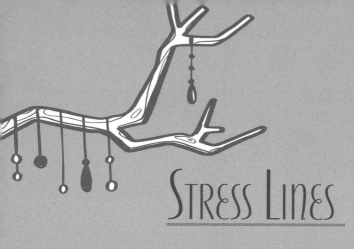

STRESS LINES

Most people have a couple of fine lines running across the primal home and body quadrant, so ignore these. These lines are worth mentioning if you see five or more deep horizontal lines in this area.

- **You may be feeling quite stressed at the moment, or perhaps life is a bit chaotic.**
- **The more uncertainty there is in your life, the more these lines are likely to appear.**
- **They will soften and disappear as the stress is dealt with.**

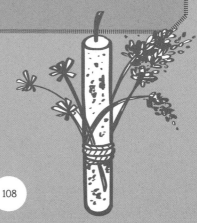

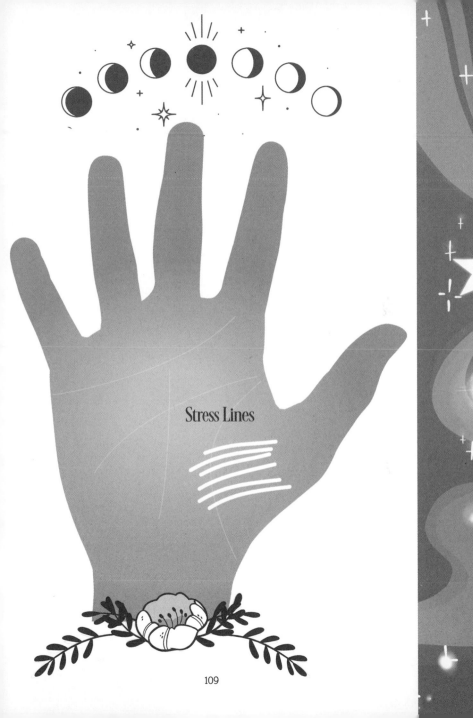

Stress Lines

Intensity Line

This line is quite common. It's a delicate, straight line in the sea of subconscious area.

- You find it difficult to relax and constantly seek excitement and movement.
- You have lots of energy and a real spark that pushes you to do daring things.
- Often, you'll find this line in parachutists, motorcyclists, racing drivers, and skiers!

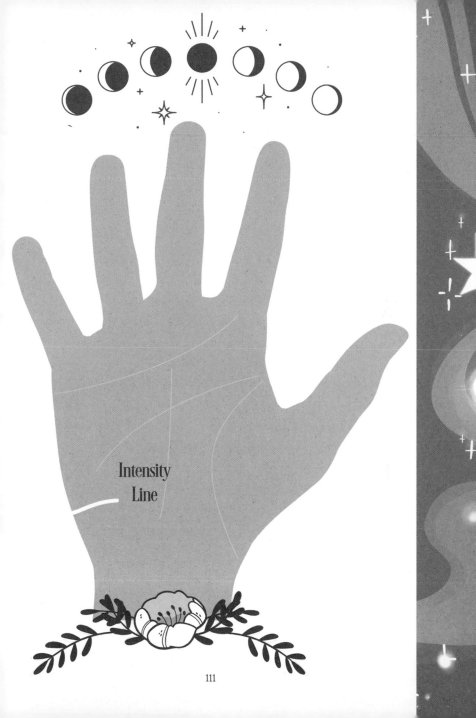

Intensity
Line

Via Lascivia

This line is found in the same place as the intensity line, but it's strongly curved instead of straight and often in a broken-up formation. Often it can run all the way to the life line.

- **Your immune system is likely to be very responsive. This means that you are likely to have allergies or lots of colds.**
- **You may also find that you have one or two phobias—such as fear of water, heights, or spiders!**

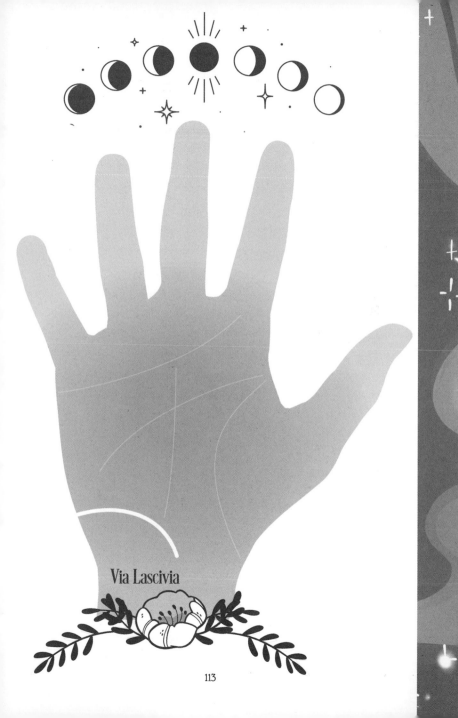

Via Lascivia

Reading Your Friends' Palms

GUIDED READING

Now it's time to put everything you have learned together!
These hands belong to a right-handed girl called Aisha. She
has put her inked palms down on paper so the right hand
will show up as if it is a left-hand outline and vice versa.
Study the pictures, then follow the questions and answers on
the following pages to read her palms.

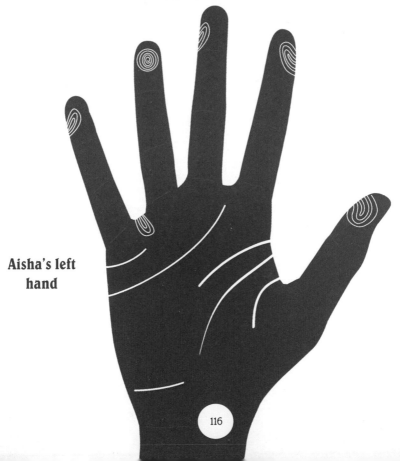

**Aisha's left
hand**

Remember, when you are reading someone's palms, you are looking for the unusual—the things that make them stand out! If they have common prints and patterns, these do not need to be discussed.

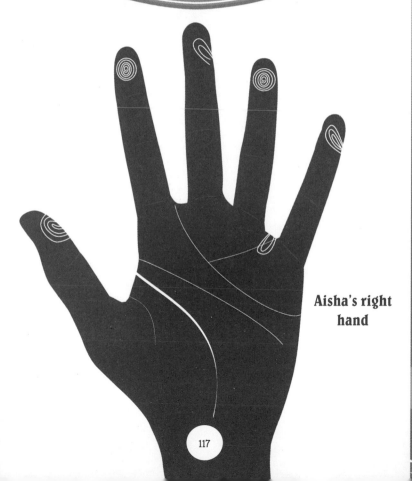

Aisha's right hand

117

START WITH THE PALMS …

- Look at the hand shape. What does this tell you?
- The skin texture is papery. What does this tell you?
- The fingers and thumb are stiff and only move a little when you pull against them. What does this tell you?

Answers

- Aisha has a rectangular palm with long fingers, so these are water hands. She might seem moody, but deep down she is kind and caring. She is artistic and loves magic and mystery.
- Paper texture skin is fairly common. Aisha can seem distant, and prefers to connect with other people through books, computers, and phones.
- Stiff thumbs and fingers show that Aisha is strong-willed and has an inflexible mind set.

NOW LOOK AT THE FINGERS ...

- Start with the mirror finger. Is it long or short or average? What does this tell you? What print pattern can you see? Compare the active/passive hands. What does this mean?
- Now the wall finger. Is it long or short or average? What print pattern can you see? What does this mean?
- Now the peacock finger. Is this long or short or average? What print pattern can you see? What does this mean?
- Now the antenna finger. Is this long or short or average? What print pattern can you see? What does this mean?
- Look at the thumb. Is this long or short or average? What print pattern can you see? What does this mean?

Answers

- The mirror fingers on both Aisha's hands are very long, which shows that she can be overly assertive. The prints are a whorl on the active finger and a radial loop on the passive one. These are opposites, showing a conflict between her private and public personalities. She is independent on the outside, but on the inside she is keen to please other people.
- The wall fingers are long, which means Aisha has a serious attitude to work and family. The prints are ulnar loops. These are the most common, so there's no need to discuss them.
- The peacock fingers are short in comparison with the mirror ones, meaning Aisha is not too concerned with popularity. The whorls show that she has creative tastes in clothes and music.
- The antenna finger is slightly long. Aisha has natural language skills. She finds it easy to talk to all sorts of different people about all sorts of different things. The prints are ulnar loops. These are the most common, so there's no need to discuss them.
- Aisha's thumbs are of average length, and both have loops. These are the most common, so there's no need to discuss them.

EXAMINE THE FOUR MAIN LINES...

- Start with the life line. What does it tell you? Are there any differences between the active and passive hands?
- Look at the heart line. What does it tell you? Are there any differences between the active and passive hands?
- Look at the head line. What does it tell you? Are there any differences between the active and passive hands?
- Look at the fate line. What does it tell you? Are there any differences between the active and passive hands?

Answers

- The life line has the bottom section missing on the active hand and it's even shorter on the passive. This shows that Aisha is a little insecure, but also strongly motivated to have a respected and well-paying career.

- The head lines are clear and straight on both palms, but the active hand's headline is much longer. The length difference shows that Aisha used to find it hard to commit to any one thing but this is beginning to change as she gets older. The straightness of the lines shows that she is a rational thinker, and the head line is separated from the life line by a large gap, showing that she is ambitious.

- The heart line is clear, curved, and ends between the mirror and wall fingers. This indicates an expressive, romantic person who finds it easy to connect with others.

- The fate line is fragmented and formed from several fine lines. This shows a lack of clarity about goals, direction, and character. It's likely Aisha still hasn't worked out exactly what she wants from life yet.

FINALLY, LOOK AT THE MINOR LINES.

• What minor lines can you see? What do they mean? Are there any differences between the active and passive hands?

Minor lines checklist:
- Sun line
- Children's lines
- Girdle of Venus
- Health line
- Intuition line
- Relationship line
- Ring of Jupiter
- Teacher's square
- Samaritan lines
- Companion lines
- Aspiration lines
- Mars line
- Stress lines
- Intensity line
- Via Lascivia

Answers

- There's a long relationship line on the passive hand, an intensity line on the passive hand and a Mars line on both hands. The relationship line suggests Aisha can find it difficult to trust people. The intensity line shows she's got a lot of energy to burn, and the Mars line shows a competitive streak! It's likely that Aisha enjoys sports where she can let off steam and challenge herself.

Top Tips

Here are some things to remember when you are reading
a friend's palm.

- Breathe deeply, speak softly, and take your time.

- Remember to be tactful, sensitive, and alert to the
  words that you use. You don't want to say something
  that will worry or upset them.

- Giving a reading can be stressful if your friend's
  expectations are too high. Let them know that you are
  not going to be able to tell them the name of their
  future crush or their cat's birthday!

- Explain that you aren't going to make scary predictions.
  You are going to talk about their deeper personality
  and reveal aspects of their true self.

- Never rush. Wait until you've looked at all aspects of
  the palm before you make any sweeping statements.

- Always examine both hands carefully and note any
  differences. These are important because they explain
  contradictory parts of your friend's personality.

- Look for the good in every issue you raise. Remember that every single pattern on the palm has good and bad aspects.

- Let your friend join in the conversation. This way, they can feel part of the process and you can get feedback on your reading.

A good palm reading is like holding up a mirror to your soul and there is enormous power, magic, and possibility in the process. Huge potential for change emerges when we truly understand ourselves.

"Magic is believing in yourself, if you can do that, you can make anything happen."

JOHANN WOLFGANG VON GOETHE

Other titles in the series:
Spells * Crystals * Astrology